BLACK HISTORY LEGENDS

Engineering, Civil Rights, Medicine, and Finance

By

Terri Whitmire

Published in the United States
by Writer's Tablet Publishing Agency
Marietta, Georgia
WritersTabletAgency.com

Black History Legends
Copyright © 2021 by Terri Whitmire
ISBN: 978-0-578-28304-3

All rights reserved. No part of this publication may be reproduced, distributed, or transmitted in any form or by any means, including photocopying, recording, or other electronic or mechanical methods, without the prior written permission of the publisher, except in the case of brief quotations embodied in critical reviews and certain other noncommercial uses permitted by copyright law.

Writer's Tablet Publishing Agency
Marietta, Georgia
www.WritersTabletAgency.com

Printed in the United States of America

Table of Contents

INTRODUCTION 1

ENGINEERING 3

    Lonnie G. Johnson 4

    Roy L. Clay 5

    Dr. Shirley Jackson 6

    Lisa Gelobter 7

    Emmit McHenry 8

    Otis Boykin 9

    Dr. Mark Dean 10

    William Fauntroy 11

    Ron McNair 12

    Gerald "Jerry" Lawson 13

CIVIL RIGHTS 15

    John Robert Lewis 16

    Nannie Helen Burroughs 17

    Fannie Lou Hamer 18

    Cornel West 19

    Dr. Dorothy Height 20

    Adam Clayton Powell 21

    Cordy "C.T." Tindell Vivian 22

    Harry Belafonte 23

    Alfred "Al" Sharpton Jr. 24

    Esmerelda Simmons 25

MEDICINE ... 27
- Daniel Hale Williams ... 28
- Rebecca Lee Crumpler ... 29
- Alexa Irene Canady ... 30
- Charles Drew ... 31
- Patricia Bath ... 32
- Dr. James McCune Smith ... 33
- Dr. Robert Boyd ... 34
- Leonidas Harris Berry ... 35
- Jocelyn Elders ... 36
- Mary Eliza Mahoney ... 37

FINANCE ... 39
- Norman L. McGhee Sr. ... 40
- Maggie Lena Walker ... 41
- Phyllis Ann Wallace ... 42
- Abram Lincoln Harris ... 43
- Joseph L. Searles III ... 44
- Valerie Mosley ... 45
- Madam C. J. Walker ... 46
- Anthony Overton ... 47
- Lauren Simmons ... 48
- Jamila Souffrant ... 49

Introduction

For centuries, black people have used their knowledge, abilities, and tenacity to create a better life for themselves and their communities. Unfortunately, many of their accomplishments were ignored or, worse yet, stolen. This book of legends includes well-known and lesser-known blacks who have made an indelible mark on our society and deserve recognition. This collection was curated for today's and future generations to see the excellence that exists and recognize they too can flourish.

Engineering

Engineering

LONNIE G. JOHNSON
1949 - _____

Inventor, Aerospace Engineer, and Entrepreneur

Lonnie Johnson was born on October 6, 1949, in Mobile, Alabama.

- His father was a World War II veteran, and his mother worked as a nurse's aide.
- Lonnie has four siblings.
- Lonnie Johnson is married with four children.

✸ ACCOMPLISHMENTS

- Lonnie Johnson invented the Super Soaker water gun.
- Johnson was the only black student in his high school science fair. He created a robot he named "Linex," and took home first prize.
- Johnson was awarded the Air Force Achievement Medal, the Air Force Commendation Medal, and breakthrough Award from the science magazine, Popular Mechanics.
- Lonnie Johnson worked for NASA in the Jet Propulsion Laboratory. He worked on the Galileo mission to Jupiter, the Mars Observer project, the Cassini mission to Saturn, and the stealth bomber program.
- He earned multiple awards from NASA for his spacecraft control systems.
- He was inducted into the State of Alabama Engineering Hall of Fame in 2011.

✸ EDUCATION

- Tuskegee University, bachelor's degree in mechanical engineering
- Tuskegee University, master's degree in nuclear engineering

✸ INTERESTING FACTS

Lonnie Johnson's father was a skilled handyman who taught his six children about electricity and how to build their own toys. The idea to create his famous Super Soaker occurred while he was working on an eco-friendly heat pump when he accidentally shot a stream of water across the bathroom where he was experimenting. The Super Soaker is now approaching close to $1 billion in sales. In February 2013, Johnson filed suit against Hasbro after discovering he was underpaid royalties for the Super Soaker and several Nerf line toys. In November 2013, Johnson was awarded nearly $73 million in royalties from Hasbro Inc. Johnson considers a robot that he built in high school one of his top three inventions, along with the Super Soaker and his work for the Galileo project. Johnson currently has two technology-development companies: Excellatron Solid State, LLC and Johnson Electro-Mechanical Systems (JEMS).

Engineering

ROY L. CLAY
1929 - _____

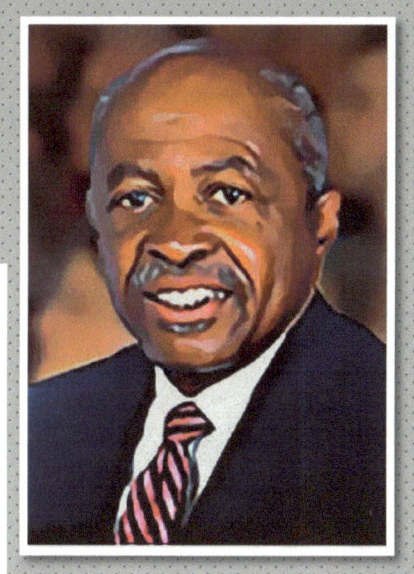

Scientist and Inventor

Roy Clay was born in 1929 in Kinloch, Missouri.

- Clay was married to Virginia Clay.
- They have three sons.

ACCOMPLISHMENTS

- Roy Clay was one of the first African Americans to graduate from Saint Louis University with a bachelor's degree.
- He taught himself to code, and by 1958 was a programmer at Lawrence Livermore National Laboratory.
- He created a radiation tracking system to study the aftermath of a nuclear explosion.
- He was a founding member of the computer division at Hewlett-Packard, where he helped launch and lead the Computer Science division in 1965.
- He served as the first African American on the Palo Alto, California, City Council in 1973.
- He started his own firm, ROD-L Electronics, which set the standard for electronic-safety equipment.

EDUCATION

- St. Louis University, bachelor's degree in mathematics

INTERESTING FACTS

While in college, Clay wanted to become a baseball player. At an interview for McDonnell Aircraft Corporation, Clay was taken aside and told, "Mr. Clay, I'm very sorry, we don't hire professional Negroes." Clay became even more determined. He worked as a schoolteacher when he first graduated from college because he struggled to find a job in the technology field. He went on to develop software to measure how radiation would spread after an atomic explosion. Mr. Clay is a community leader in youth development and has worked tirelessly for over 35 years in Silicon Valley. After his wife, Virginia, died, he founded the Virginia Clay/Unity Care Annual Golf Classic to honor her memory and to promote success for young minorities. He has been inducted into the Silicon Valley Engineering Hall of Fame.

Engineering

DR. SHIRLEY JACKSON
1946 - _____

Physicist

Dr. Jackson was born to Beatrice and George Jackson on August 5, 1946, in Washington, DC.

Shirley Jackson is married to Morris A. Washington, a physics professor.

They have one son.

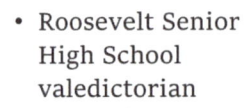

ACCOMPLISHMENTS

- Shirley Jackson is the first African-American woman to have earned a doctorate at the Massachusetts Institute of Technology.
- She is also the second African-American woman in the United States to earn a doctorate in nuclear physics.
- Dr. Jackson conducted breakthrough basic scientific research that enabled others to invent the portable fax, the touch-tone telephone, solar cells, fiber optic cables, and the technology behind caller I.D. and call waiting.
- Jackson is the president of Rensselaer Polytechnic.
- In 1995 President Bill Clinton appointed Jackson to serve as Chairman of the US Nuclear Regulatory Commission (NRC), becoming the first woman and first African American to hold that position.

EDUCATION

- Roosevelt Senior High School valedictorian
- Massachusetts Institute of Technology (MIT), bachelor's degree, master's degree, and PhD

INTERESTING FACTS

When Jackson was at MIT, she was one of fewer than 20 African American students and the only black student studying Theoretical Physics. A 2015 *Time Magazine* article cited Jackson as the highest-paid college president. She "took home a base salary of $945,000 plus another $276,474 in bonuses, $31,874 in nontaxable benefits, and $5.8 million in deferred compensation, for a stunning $7.1 million in total. She was featured on the PBS show *Finding Your Roots* Season 6 Episode 7, where she is noted as one of the leading global pioneers in science, all while knowing little about her ancestry.

Engineering

LISA GELOBTER
1971 - _____

Computer Scientist and Technology Executive

Lisa Gelobter was born in 1971.

- Her father is Jewish and a Holocaust survivor.
- Her mother is black and from the Caribbean.

✺ ACCOMPLISHMENTS

- Lisa Gelobter was the Chief Digital Officer of the U.S. Department of Education. She led this startup at The White House, using design and technology to deliver better services to the American people.
- She has been recognized for her programs that help fight racial discrimination in the workplace.
- She was a part of the senior management team to launch Hulu, the popular online video streaming service.
- Gelobter also acted as the Chief Digital Officer for BET (Black Entertainment Television) Networks.
- She created the animation used to produce GIFs.

✺ EDUCATION

- Brown University, bachelor of science in computer science (at just 20 years old).

✺ INTERESTING FACTS

Lisa Gelobter worked hard to attend college, which she paid for herself by working 40 hours a week while in school. Lisa Gelobter served as the Chief Digital Service Officer for the Department of Education, where she worked on the team that redesigned the College Scorecard. This rating system shows graduation rates, post-college earnings, and student debt levels for universities across the country. Gelobter is the CEO and co-founder of tEquitable, a technology-driven company focusing on making the workplace more inclusive. Gelobter is one of Inc.'s 100 Women Building America's Most Innovative and Ambitious Businesses and was named one of Fast Company's Most Creative People. When asked what superhero she would like to be, she answered, "Shuri from *Black Panther* because she's a black female scientist."

Engineering

EMMIT McHENRY
1943 - ____

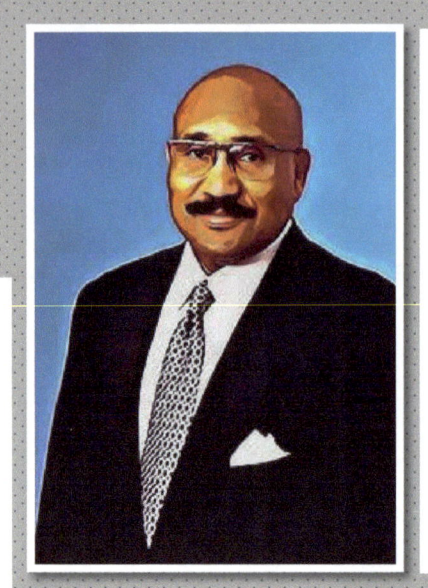

Technologist and Entrepreneur

McHenry was born to Drucie and John Saunders Chase on July 12, 1943, in Forrest City, Arkansas.

- His father was an architect and his mother a teacher.

ACCOMPLISHMENTS

- Emmit McHenry is the founder, chairman, and CEO of NetCom Solutions International, Inc. *Enterprise Magazine* ranked his company 10th in African American-owned business.
- McHenry made the internet accessible to ordinary people who do not understand computer science by inventing .com, .net, .edu, and .gov. This allowed people to surf the internet.
- McHenry was a Lieutenant in the US Marine Corps
- He received the Chairman's Award from the Historically Black Colleges and Universities Foundation.

EDUCATION

- The University of Denver, bachelor of science in communication
- Northwestern University, master's degree in communications
- Honorary doctorate from Shaw University

INTERESTING FACTS

McHenry worked on a project creating the world wide web, which was initially a U.S. government Cold War project. McHenry was tech-wise, but because he was black, it was difficult to find financial investments to fund his technology ideas. So he and his partners mortgaged their properties and used credit cards to finance it. McHenry's first technology company, Network Solutions, was ahead of its time. He received $1 million for their first contract, but that wasn't enough for his growing business. He underestimated its future value and sold the company for much less than what it would be worth. Under his leadership as CEO of Chantilly-based NetCom Solutions, the company made $76 million in revenue. He knew multiparty computer gaming would be huge and now looks forward to having holograms in his house.

Engineering

OTIS BOYKIN
1920 - 1982

Inventor and Engineer

Otis Boykin was born to Sarah and Walter Boykin on August 29, 1920, in Dallas, Texas.

- His father was a carpenter and later became a preacher. His mother was a maid.

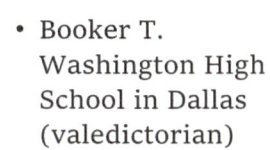

✨ ACCOMPLISHMENTS

- Otis Boykin invented a control unit for the pacemaker that allows the device to work more precisely.
- IBM began using Boykin's new resistors in their computers, and the United States military applied the technology to the production of guided missiles.
- Boykin started his own company, Boykin-Fruth Inc.
- Boykin patented as many as 26 devices.
- Boykin was inducted into the National Inventors Hall of Fame.

✨ EDUCATION

- Booker T. Washington High School in Dallas (valedictorian)
- Fisk University, bachelor's degree
- Illinois Institute of Technology in Chicago (he completed two years)

✨ INTERESTING FACTS

Otis Boykin's first job was at Majestic Radio and TV Corporation. He began to invent products on his own, including a wire precision resistor used in televisions and radios. Sadly, Boykin's mother died of heart failure, which inspired him to improve the design of the pacemaker. Before his invention, pacemakers were outside of the body and had to be plugged into the wall.

Engineering

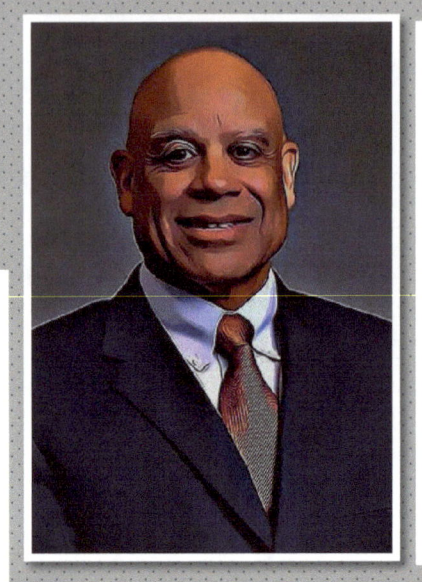

DR. MARK DEAN
1957 - _____

Computer Scientist and Engineer

Mark Dean was born on March 2, 1957, in Jefferson City, Tennessee

- His father worked as a supervisor with the Tennessee Valley Authority.

ACCOMPLISHMENTS

- Mark Dean invented the color P.C. monitor.
- Dean invented Industry Standard Architect (ISA) systems bus that allowed disk drives, printers, and monitors to be plugged directly into computers.
- He has more than 20 patents associated with his name.
- Dean led a team of engineers at IBM's Austin, Texas, lab to create the first gigahertz chip—a revolutionary piece of technology that can do a billion calculations a second.
- He was named an IBM Fellow, the first African American ever to receive the honor.
- Dean was inducted into the National Inventors Hall of Fame.
- He is the Vice President of Systems in IBM Research.

EDUCATION

- The University of Tennessee, bachelor's degree in engineering
- Florida Atlantic University, master's degree in electrical engineering
- Stanford University, a doctorate in electrical engineering

INTERESTING FACTS

A white friend from school asked Dean if he was really black. Dean said his friend had concluded he was too smart to be black. As one of IBM's "idea men," he came up with the idea of an "electronic tablet." Dean was frustrated by the bulkiness of newspapers and wanted to create a small, magazine-sized device that could download any electronic text, including from newspapers and books. He wanted to be able to write on this device and have the text recognized by the device. It would also be voice-activated and even talk back. But while the tablet did accomplish all of those things, Dean would like the price to be cheaper, allowing every student to have one instead of textbooks.

Engineering

WILLIAM FAUNTROY
1926 -____

Pilot and Activist

William T. Fauntroy, Jr. was born to Ethel and William Thomas Fauntroy on March 26, 1926, in the District of Columbia.

- William Fauntroy's father was a clerk in the U.S. Patent Office.
- His mother was a homemaker.
- Fauntroy was the fourth of seven children.
- His wife is Dorothy Fauntroy. They have two children.

ACCOMPLISHMENTS

- William Fauntroy served in the Army Air Corps.
- After basic training, he was assigned to the Tuskegee Army Air Field for training as a single-engine pilot.
- William Fauntroy was part of "Red Tails," famous black pilots who became heroes during World War II.
- He was the first African-American civil engineer to be hired by the National Capital Transportation Agency (NCTA).
- Mr. Fauntroy was the urban planner for a portion of the District of Columbia's subway system.
- He is a lifetime member of the American Society of Civil Engineers.

EDUCATION

- Howard University, bachelor of science degree in civil engineering

INTERESTING FACTS

Fauntroy played himself in the films *A Defining Moment* (2011) and *Resurrecting Moton Field* (2009). These documentaries about his life and his fellow Tuskegee Airmen told the story of young black pilots who volunteered to become America's first black military airmen (Red Tails). Those who possessed the physical and mental qualifications were accepted for aviation cadet training and trained to become pilots, navigators, or bombardiers. As a Tuskegee Airman, Fauntroy's nickname was 'Baby Soldier' because he was only 5 foot 4 and a half, and 5 foot 4 was the minimum height for pilots.

Engineering

RON McNAIR
1950 - 1986

✱ACCOMPLISHMENTS

- Ron McNair was selected as one of 35 applicants from a pool of 10,000 for the NASA astronaut program.
- McNair flew as a mission specialist on STS-41-B aboard Challenger from February 3 to February 11, 1984, becoming the second African American to fly in space. McNair and the four other crew members logged 191 hours in space on the eight-day mission. Challenger made 128 orbits around the Earth on that trip.
- McNair studied laser physics with many authorities in the field.
- He published several papers in the areas of lasers and molecular spectroscopy and gave many presentations in the United States and abroad.
- McNair was awarded the Congressional Space Medal of Honor in 2004.
- McNair has a crater on the moon named after him.

Astronaut and Physicist

Ron McNair was born to Pearl and Carl McNair on October 21, 1950, in Lake City, South Carolina.

- He had two brothers.
- He married Cheryl Moore and they had two children.

✱EDUCATION

- North Carolina Agricultural and Technical State University, bachelor of science degree in engineering physics (magna cum laude)
- Massachusetts Institute of Technology, PhD in LASER Physics (with honors)
- He received four honorary doctorates.

✱INTERESTING FACTS

When Ron McNair was nine years old, he refused to leave the segregated Lake City Public Library without being allowed to check out his books. After the police and his mother were called, he was allowed to borrow books from the library. This same building is now called The Ronald E. McNair Life History Center. McNair was a 6th-degree black belt in taekwondo and an accomplished saxophonist. He received numerous awards, including a Ford Foundation Fellow, National Fellowship Fund Fellow, NATO Fellow, Omega Psi Phi Scholar of the Year Award, Distinguished Alumni Award, Distinguished National Scientist Award, Friend of Freedom Award, and Who's Who Among Black Americans. Sadly, Ron McNair was one of the seven astronauts killed in the January 28, 1986 explosion of the space shuttle Challenger.

Engineering

GERALD "JERRY" LAWSON
1940 - 2011

✹ ACCOMPLISHMENTS

- Jerry Lawson led the team that pioneered the commercial game cartridge.
- Most game systems had the game programming built into the game hardware, which could not be removed. Lawson and his team improved the technology so that games could be stored as software that could be inserted and removed from a console unit repeatedly.
- Lawson founded Videosoft, Inc., a video game development company that made software for the Atari 2600.
- He was the only black engineer in the Homebrew Computer Club, a group of early computer hobbyists that included many industry legends, including Apple founders Steve Jobs.
- He has been called the "Father of Modern Gaming."
- Lawson was honored as an industry pioneer for his work on the game cartridge concept by the International Game Developers Association (IGDA)

Engineer and Game Designer

Jerry Lawson was born to Mannings and Blanton Lawson in Brooklyn, New York City, on December 1, 1940.

- His father was a longshoreman interested in science, while his mother worked for the city.
- Lawson was married with two children.

✹ EDUCATION

- Queens College and City College of New York (he did not graduate from either)

✹ INTERESTING FACTS

Jerry Lawson attended an elementary school composed of 99% white students, where his first-grade teacher inspired him to become a scientist. While in high school, he earned money by repairing television sets. At 13, Jerry Lawson built radios and researched how to start his own licensed radio station. Later, he created the arcade game Demolition Derby in his garage. Lawson's work allowed people to play a variety of games in their homes and paved the way for systems such as the Atari 2600, Nintendo, Xbox, and PlayStation. He was featured in the first episode of the Netflix limited-series documentary *High Score*, with his story told by his children Karen and Anderson.

14

Civil Rights

Civil Rights

JOHN ROBERT LEWIS
1961 - 2020

American Statesman, Civil Rights Leader, United States Representative

John Lewis was born on February 21, 1940, near Troy, Alabama. He had a happy childhood though he had to work hard to assist his sharecropper parents.
- Married Lilian Miles
- He had one adopted son, John Miles Lewis
- He had five siblings: three brothers and two sisters

ACCOMPLISHMENTS

- John Lewis received the Presidential Medal of Freedom in 2011.
- He participated in the Freedom Rides of 1961.
- Lewis was the chairman of the Student Nonviolent Coordinating Committee.
- He led the March from Selma to Montgomery, Alabama, crossing the Edmund Pettus Bridge, known as "Bloody Sunday" after racist state troopers attacked Lewis and other marchers. This attack, seen by the world, sped up the passage of 1965's Voting Rights Act.
- Lewis was elected to the United States House of Representatives in 1986 and served 17 terms.
- He was the recipient of The Profile in Courage Award.

EDUCATION

- American Baptist College, bachelor's degree in theology.
- Fisk University, bachelor of arts in religion and philosophy

INTERESTING FACTS

While in college at The American Baptist Theological Seminary, he became an ordained minister and learned about nonviolent protests. Along with Martin Luther King Jr., John Lewis was one of the "Big Six" leaders of the Civil Rights Movement. He marched, boycotted, and organized sit-ins at segregated lunch counters. In the 1960s, John Lewis created a series of graphic novels about his work in the Civil Rights Movement. In 2016, he won the National Book Award for the third installment in the series March: Book Three, the first time a graphic novel has received the honor. John Lewis met his wife Lilian at a New Year's Eve party hosted by civil rights leader Xernona Clayton in 1967. Sadly, after a long illness, she died on December 31, 2012, New Year's Eve.

Civil Rights

NANNIE HELEN BURROUGHS
1879 - 1961

Educator, Religious Leader, Social Activist, Women's Suffrage Activist

Born on May 2, 1879, in Orange, Virginia.

Nannie's parents, John and Jennie Burroughs, were both former slaves. They had skills and capacities that enabled them to start building wealth by the time the war ended and freed them.
- When she was seven years old, her father, a farmer, and Baptist preacher, died.
- She and her mother moved to D.C. in 1883.

✸ ACCOMPLISHMENTS

- Nannie Helen Burroughs started The Christian Banner Newspaper.
- She wrote as a columnist for The Pittsburgh Courier, an African-American newspaper.
- Nannie was famous for delivering a speech at the National Convention entitled, "How the Sisters Are Hindered from Helping."
- She was the leader of the Woman's Convention.
- She was the keynote speaker to 10,000 attendees at the First Baptist World Alliance Congress held in London, England.
- Nannie was appointed by President Hoover as the chairman of White House Programs for home building and ownerships.

✸ EDUCATION

- Eckstein-Norton University
- Honorary master of arts degree in 1907

✸ INTERESTING FACTS

Nannie Helen Burroughs tried to find a teaching job in Washington, D.C., but because of racism, she was unable to, despite her thorough education and preparation. While the school system did hire black teachers at the time, it preferred light-skinned ones. When she realized she would not be hired, she used this disappointment and founded The National Training School for Black Women and Girls in 1909. At 26 years old she became their first president. She never married but devoted her time to this school, which was later renamed the Nannie Burroughs School. Nannie Helen Burroughs lived in a time when black people started creating wealth just after slavery. She supported buying from black businesses and wanted to build a strong community. In 1975, The mayor of D.C. declared May 10th as Nannie Helen Burroughs day.

Civil Rights

FANNIE LOU HAMER
1917 - 1977

American Voting and Women's Rights Activist, Community Organizer, Civil Rights Activist

Fannie Lou Hammer was born to Lou Ella and James Townsend on October 6, 1917, in Montgomery County, Mississippi.

- She was the youngest of 20 children.
- She grew up in poverty.
- At age six, she picked cotton with her family.

✶ ACCOMPLISHMENTS

- Fannie Lou Hamer was the organizer of the Student Non-Violent Coordinating Committee and in 1962, she led 17 volunteers to register to vote.
- In 1964, she founded the Mississippi Freedom Democratic Party, which challenged the local Democratic Party's efforts to block black people from participating.
- She was a member of Mississippi's first integrated delegation.
- In 1964, Hamer helped organize Freedom Summer, which brought hundreds of black and white college students to help with African-American voter registration.
- In 1969, she launched the Freedom Farm Cooperative, buying up land that blacks could own and farm.

✶ EDUCATION

- She left school at 12 years old to go to work.

✶ INTERESTING FACTS

For protesting racial injustice, she and several women were brutally beaten, leaving Hamer with lifelong injuries from a blood clot in her eye, kidney damage, and leg damage. In June of 1963, after successfully registering to vote, Hamer and several other Black women were arrested for sitting in a "whites-only" bus station restaurant in Charleston, South Carolina. At age 44, Fannie went in to have a tumor removed and was illegally given a hysterectomy. This was frequently done to black women to prevent them from having children. Fannie and her husband later adopted two daughters. With the assistance of donors (including famed singer Harry Belafonte), she purchased 640 acres of land and launched a co-op store, boutique, and sewing enterprise. She single-handedly ensured that 200 units of low-income housing were built—many still exist in Ruleville today.

Civil Rights

CORNEL WEST
1953 - _____

Political Activist, Author, and University Professor

Cornel Ronald West was born to Irene and Clifton Louis West Jr. on June 2, 1953, in Tulsa, Oklahoma

- He has three siblings
- His mother taught elementary school, and his father worked as a civilian administrator for the U.S. Air Force.

ACCOMPLISHMENTS

- Cornel West was the first African American to graduate from Princeton University with a PhD in philosophy.
- He taught at Harvard University, New York Theological Seminary, The University of Paris, Princeton, and Yale Divinity School.
- In 1982, West's book, Prophesy Deliverance: An Afro-American Revolutionary Christianity, was published.
- He is the recipient of more than 20 honorary degrees and an American Book Award
- He has written or contributed to over 20 published books.

EDUCATION

- Harvard University, bachelor degree (earned in just three years)
- Princeton University, master's degree and doctorate in philosophy

INTERESTING FACTS

Cornel West's political activism dates back to his childhood when he participated in civil rights demonstrations with his family in Sacramento, California. While Cornell West was teaching at Yale University, he took part in protests against South Africa's apartheid regime and was subsequently arrested. In 2003, West made his big-screen debut in *The Matrix Reloaded*. He also appeared in the final film of the Matrix trilogy, *The Matrix Revolutions*. In 2001, West released his first album, *Sketches of My Culture*. The album *Street Knowledge* followed. In 2007, West released *Never Forget: A Journey of Revelations*. This album included collaborations with Prince, Talib Kweli, Jill Scott, Andre 3000, KRS-One, and the late Gerald Levert. In 2010, he completed recordings with the Cornel West Theory Band.

Civil Rights

DR. DOROTHY HEIGHT
1912 - 2010

Civil Rights and Women's Rights Activist

Dorothy Irene Height was born to James and Fannie Height on March 24, 1912, in Richmond, Virginia.

- Her dad was a building contractor.
- Her mom was a nurse.
- When she was five years old, she moved with her family to Rankin, Pennsylvania.

ACCOMPLISHMENTS

- Dorothy Height worked with the National Council of Negro Women (NCNW), focusing on restructuring the criminal justice system.
- In 1957, she became the fourth president of the NCNW, where she served for 40 years.
- In 1989, she received the Citizens Medal Award.
- She was honored with the Presidential Medal of Freedom and The Congressional Gold Medal.
- Dr. Height was inducted into the Democracy Hall of Fame International in 2004.
- In the 1990s, she drew young people into her cause in the war against drugs, illiteracy, and unemployment.

EDUCATION

- New York University, bachelor's degree in education and master's degree in psychology.
- She received 24 honorary degrees

INTERESTING FACTS

Young Dorothy was a skilled speaker. In high school, she won an oratory competition, which awarded her a college scholarship. After working as a social worker, Height joined the Harlem YWCA staff in 1937. There, she met Mary McLeod Bethune and Eleanor Roosevelt. Former United States Presidents Lyndon B. Johnson, Dwight D. Eisenhower, and First Lady Eleanor Roosevelt often asked Dr. Height for advice on political issues. She played a major role in planning the March on Washington but was not allowed to speak. She and other female activists noticed the gender discrimination (sexism) in the Civil Rights Movement, which she sought to correct. Dr. Height became a visiting professor at the University of Delhi, India, and the Black Women's Federation of South Africa. In celebration of the 102nd anniversary of her birthday, Google featured a doodle with a portrait of Dr. Height.

Civil Rights

ADAM CLAYTON POWELL
1908 - 1972

Pastor and Congressman

Adam Clayton Powell was born to Mattie and Adam Clayton Powell Sr. on November 29, 1908, in New Haven, Connecticut.

- His father was a pastor.
- He had one older sister.
- His parents were mixed-race, with African and European ancestry.

✱ ACCOMPLISHMENTS

- Adam Clayton Powell became the first African American elected to the New York City Council.
- He was elected to the U.S. House of Representatives, representing a newly formed congressional district in Harlem.
- Powell headed the "Don't buy where you can't work" movement, which encouraged black people to boycott businesses that expected black people to spend money but would not hire them. This movement was successfully able to open up jobs to African Americans at New York stores, utility companies, and city buses.

✱ EDUCATION

- Colgate University, bachelor's degree
- Columbia University, master of art in religious education

✱ INTERESTING FACTS

Due to his father's achievements, Powell grew up in a wealthy household in New York City. Adam was born with hazel eyes, light skin, and blond hair, such that he could pass for white. While in college, he used his white appearance to escape racial restrictions. Powell traveled to Ghana with Dr. Martin Luther King, Jr. in 1957 to celebrate Ghana's independence. He also helped to create a law that prevents the government from giving money to segregated colleges and universities. The law was never passed, but it eventually became a part of the Civil Rights Act of 1964 and was named the Powell Amendment.

Civil Rights

CORDY "C.T." TINDELL VIVIAN
1924 - 2020

Minister and Author

C.T. Vivian was born to Euzetta and Robert Cordie on July 30, 1924, in Boonville, Missouri.

- He was an only child.
- His parents divorced when he was young.
- Vivian was raised by his mother and grandmother, Annie Woods Tindell.
- He married Octavia Geans.

ACCOMPLISHMENTS

- Cordy C.T. Vivian served as the national director of affiliates for the Southern Christian Leadership Conference.
- He helped organize the first sit-ins in Nashville in 1960 and the first civil rights march in 1961.
- Vivian founded the Black Action Strategies & Information Center (BASIC) in Atlanta to help with race relations in the workplace.
- He spoke publicly at many conferences and offered workshops around the world, including the United Nations.
- He founded and incorporated the C.T. Vivian Leadership Institute, Inc. (CTVLI) to create a model leadership culture in Atlanta, Georgia.

EDUCATION

- Western Illinois (he did not graduate.)
- American Baptist Theological Seminary
- Honorary doctorate from the New School for Social Research

INTERESTING FACTS

In 1930, his mother and grandmother moved to Macomb, Illinois, because the schools were not segregated, and the city had a college. His first professional job was recreation director for the Carver Community Center in Peoria, Illinois. There, Vivian participated in his first sit-in demonstrations, which successfully integrated Barton's Cafeteria in 1947. While giving a speech, he was punched in the face on the county courthouse steps in Selma, Alabama, by a police officer. C.T. Vivian was a founder of Capital City Bank in Atlanta. C.T. Vivian was a leader in the Civil Rights Movement and a friend to Martin Luther King, Jr. He received the Presidential Medal of Freedom in 2013. Vivian died on the same day as his friend and fellow activist, John Lewis. C.T. Vivian was the first black, non-elected man to lie in state at the Georgia State Capitol.

Civil Rights

HARRY BELAFONTE
1927 - ____

Singer, Songwriter, and Activist

Harry Belafonte was born to Melvine (née Love) and Harold George Bellanfanti Sr, on March 1, 1927, in New York City.

- His birth name is Harold George Bellanfanti, Jr.
- His mother was Jamaican, a dressmaker and a house cleaner.
- His father served as a cook on a merchant ship.

ACCOMPLISHMENTS

- Harry Belafonte was a civil rights activist and a close friend to Dr. Martin Luther King Jr.
- He is a Caribbean folk singer and his album, Calypso (1956), became the first full-length album to sell one million copies. "The Banana Boat Song (Day-O)" was a huge hit.
- Belafonte won a Tony Award for his performance in the Broadway musical John Murray Anderson's Almanac.
- In the 1960s, he became the first African-American television producer.
- He received the Jean Hersholt Humanitarian Award from the Academy of Motion Picture Arts and Sciences in 2014 (The Oscars).

EDUCATION

- Harry Belafonte dropped out of high school.
- Erwin Piscator's Dramatic Workshop.

INTERESTING FACTS

Belafonte spent much of his early years in Jamaica, his mother's native country. There, he saw firsthand the oppression of black people by the English authorities. Belafonte returned to New York City's Harlem neighborhood in 1940 to live with his mother. They struggled in poverty, and Belafonte was often cared for by others while his mother worked. This anguished him. He enlisted in the U.S. Navy in 1944. He returned to New York City and worked as a janitor's assistant. His interest in acting was sparked when he attended a production at the American Negro Theater (AMT). In 2001, he went to South Africa to support the campaign against HIV/AIDS. In 2002, Africare awarded him the Bishop John T. Walker Distinguished Humanitarian Service Award.

Civil Rights

ALFRED "AL" SHARPTON JR.
1954 - _____

Civil Rights Activist, Baptist Minister, Talk Show Host, and Politician

Al Sharpton was born to Ada and Alfred Sharpton, Sr. on October 3, 1954, in Brooklyn, New York.

- His mother worked as a maid, but they were very poor and had to receive government assistance.

ACCOMPLISHMENTS

- Alfred Sharpton became an ordained minister at the age of ten.
- He established the National Youth Movement in 1971.
- Sharpton formed the National Action Network, a civil rights organization that promotes policies that benefit African Americans.
- While in high school, he became the youth director for Operation Breadbasket, a program with the Southern Christian Leadership Conference.
- During the 1980s, Sharpton became involved in many high-profile cases in the New York City area that affected the African American community and led several protests against racial discrimination.

EDUCATION

- Brooklyn College (he did not graduate.)

INTERESTING FACTS

Al Sharpton organized the One Thousand Ministers March for Justice on the 54th anniversary of the historic March on Washington in 2017. The March was to protest racism and Donald Trump. Outspoken and sometimes controversial, Sharpton has become a leading figure in the fight against racial prejudice and injustice. While facing several accusations, he remained dedicated to his activism, arranging protests and giving press conferences. During one such protest in Brooklyn's Bensonhurst neighborhood in 1991, a man stabbed Sharpton in the chest. They rushed him to the hospital. He had surgery and eventually made a full recovery. Sharpton delivered the eulogy at the funeral of George Floyd, a man who was brutally killed by police officers and whose death sparked international protests in 2020.

Civil Rights

ESMERELDA SIMMONS
1950 - _____

Civil Rights Lawyer and Activist

Esmerelda Simmons was born in 1950 in Brooklyn, New York

Her parents immigrated from St. Croix, an island that is a part of the U.S. Virgin Islands.

- Her father was an accountant, and her mother worked at the Metropolitan Museum of Art.
- She is married to Lesley Jean-Jacques. They have three children.

✸ ACCOMPLISHMENTS

- Esmeralda Simmons served in the Office for Civil Rights in the U.S. Department of Education and Assistant Attorney General for the state of New York.
- She served as the first Deputy State Commissioner of Human Rights for New York State.
- She founded the Center for Law and Social Justice at Medgar Evers College.
- In 1993, Mayor David Dinkins appointed her to the New York City Board of Education.
- In 2014, she was named a New York State Woman of Distinction.

✸ EDUCATION

- Hunter College, bachelor of arts degree
- Brooklyn Law School
- Columbia University, Remsen Fellowship

✸ INTERESTING FACTS

Esmeralda Simmons is known as one of the top influential activists still alive as of 2022. Her family went from living in public housing to being home buyers. She was one of a few black students to integrate her elementary and high school. She offers legal support to her community for various challenges, including immigration, police brutality, red-lining, community advocacy training, education, and voting rights. She is a strong advocate for quality public education for students of color. In 2018, she received the Haywood Burns Award from the New York State Bar Association.

26

Medicine

Medicine

DANIEL HALE WILLIAMS
1856 - 1931

Cardiologist and Surgeon

Daniel Hale Williams was born to Sarah and Daniel Hale Williams II on January 18, 1856, in Hollidaysburg.

- His father was black and a barber. His mother was Scotch-Irish. They did very well in establishing wealth.
- Daniel had five siblings.

✸ ACCOMPLISHMENTS

- In 1893, Dr. Williams became the first surgeon to perform open-heart surgery on a human.
- He founded Chicago's Provident Hospital, the first non-segregated hospital in the United States, and established an associated nursing school for African Americans.
- Dr. Williams moved to Washington, DC, where as Chief Surgeon of the Freedmen's Hospital, he continued his assault on health disparities by encouraging the employment of a multiracial staff and promoting the advancement of surgical procedures.
- He worked at Meharry Medical College for about 20 years, beginning in 1899.
- In 1913, he became a charter member of the American College of Surgeons.

✸ EDUCATION

- Two-year apprenticeship.
- Chicago Medical College, medical degree

✸ INTERESTING FACTS

After their father died, the Williams children were separated. Eleven-year-old Daniel was taken out of school and sent to Baltimore, MD, to work as a shoemaker's apprentice. Daniel Hale wanted to become a barber like his father, even opening his own barbershop at age 17. He tried to become a lawyer like his brother; however, after losing interest, he went to medical school. He struggled with his studies but was able to pass all of his classes. During finals week, he fell ill with smallpox, which left him with pockmarks on his nose. After graduating from medical school in 1883, he opened a practice in a well-to-do South Side Chicago neighborhood. Because heart surgery was not a widespread practice, Williams and other pioneer heart surgeons were not recognized for their work for many years. Considered a thoughtful and skilled surgeon, Dr. Williams' practice grew as he treated both black and white patients. He also worked with the Equal Rights League, a black civil rights organization active during the Reconstruction era.

Medicine

REBECCA LEE CRUMPLER
1831 - 1895

Physician and Author

Rebecca Lee Crumpler was born to Matilda and Absolum in 1831, in Delaware.

She was raised in Pennsylvania by her aunt.

- Rebecca Crumpler married Wyatt Lee, a Virginia native, and former slave.
- She had one daughter, Lizzie Sinclair Crumpler.

*Often confused with Mary Eliza Mahoney, no credible picture was found of Rebecca Lee Crumpler.

ACCOMPLISHMENTS

- Dr. Rebecca Crumpler's Book of Medical Discourses is one of the very first medical publications by an African American.
- She was the first African-American woman to earn a medical degree.
- The Rebecca Lee Society, one of the first medical societies for African-American women, was named in her honor.
- Her home on Joy Street is a stop on the Boston Women's Heritage Trail.
- She was the only black graduate from The New England Female Medical College.
- Rebecca worked with the Freedman's Bureau for the State of Virginia, helping more than 4,000,000 slaves make the stunning transition from bondage to freedom.

EDUCATION

- New England Female Medical College, medical degree

INTERESTING FACTS

Rebecca Lee Crumpler became interested in the medical field because of her aunt, who cared for sick neighbors. Rebecca used her skills to care for freed slaves who would otherwise have had no access to medical care. She was subjected to "intense racism" and sexism while practicing medicine. During this time, many men believed that a man's brain was ten percent bigger than a woman's brain on average and that a woman's job was to act submissively and be beautiful. They did not respect Rebecca Lee Crumpler and would not approve her patients' prescriptions or listen to her medical opinions. She wrote A Book of Medical Discourses in Two Parts. The first part focused on "treating the cause, prevention, and cure of infant bowel complaints." The second section contains "miscellaneous information concerning the life and growth of beings; the beginning of womanhood; also, the cause, prevention, and cure of many of the most distressing complaints of women, and youth of both sexes."

Medicine

ALEXA IRENE CANADY
1950 - ___

Medical Doctor and Neurosurgeon

Alexa Irene Canady was born to Elizabeth and Dr. Clinton Canady Jr. on November 7, 1950, in Lansing, Michigan.

- Her father was a dentist. Her mother was a teacher.
- Canady has one younger brother.

ACCOMPLISHMENTS

- Alexa Canady was the first African-American woman in the United States to become a neurosurgeon.
- She was a surgical intern at the Yale-New Haven Hospital from 1975-1976.
- In 1982, after finishing residency, Dr. Canady decided to specialize as a pediatric neurosurgeon, becoming the first African American and the first woman to do so.
- She was inducted into the Michigan Woman's Hall of Fame in 1989.
- In 1993, she received the American Medical Women's Association President's Award.
- In 1994. she received the Distinguished Service Award from Wayne State University Medical School.
- In 2002, the Detroit News named Dr. Canady Michiganer of the Year.

EDUCATION

- University of Michigan bachelor's degree in zoology.
- The University of Michigan Medical School, graduating cum laude (with honors).

INTERESTING FACTS

Canady and her younger brother were the only two African-American students in their school, where she faced prejudice. In one instance, a family member who was training in psychology tested her at a young age for intelligence. When she scored highly on the exam, her family was surprised because her grades were pretty average. They later discovered that her teacher switched her test scores with a white student to cover up her intelligence. She worked in Dr. Bloom's lab in genetics and attended a genetic counseling clinic. Alexa Canady chose to specialize in pediatrics because of her love of the children in the pediatric ward during her residency, stating, "it never ceased to amaze me how happy the children were." As a patient-focused surgeon, she was known to play video games with her pediatric patients. Dr. Canady continues to be an advocate for both her profession and diversity in medicine.

Medicine

CHARLES DREW
1904 - 1950

Surgeon and Researcher

Dr. Drew was born to Richard and Nora Burell on June 3, 1904, in Washington, DC.

- His father was a carpet layer, and his mother was trained as a teacher but never worked.
- Charles Drew had three younger siblings.

ACCOMPLISHMENTS

- Charles Drew discovered a method for the long-term storage of blood plasma. He instituted ground-breaking procedures for collecting blood and processing blood plasma.
- Drew was the assistant director for a national blood banking system, sponsored by the National Research Council and the American Red Cross. Among his innovations were mobile blood donation stations, later called "bloodmobiles."
- In June 1940, Drew received his doctor of medical science degree from Columbia, becoming the first African American to earn that degree there.
- Because of his innovative work, he received many awards and honors, including the 1942 E. S. Jones Award, an appointment to the American-Soviet Committee on Science in 1943, and an election to the International College of Surgeons.

EDUCATION

- Amherst College, bachelor's degree

- McGill University, doctor of medicine and master of surgery degrees.

- Columbia University, doctoral degree.

INTERESTING FACTS

In Washington DC, Drew attended Stevens Elementary and then Dunbar High School, which was at the time one of the best college preparatory schools—for blacks or whites—in the country. He was smart but with average grades. Instead, he concentrated on athletics. He lettered in four sports and won the James E. Walker Medal for all-around athletic performance in both his junior and senior years. He was voted "best athlete" and "most popular student." In 1928, he applied to medical school and enrolled at McGill University in Montreal, Canada. The racial segregation of the pre-Civil Rights era constrained Drew's options for medical training. Some prominent medical schools, such as Harvard, accepted a few non-white students each year, but most African Americans aspiring to medical careers attended black institutions. Graduating in 1933, Drew was second in his class. He also campaigned against the exclusion of black physicians from local medical societies, medical specialty organizations, and the American Medical Association.

Medicine

PATRICIA BATH
1942 - 2019

Ophthalmologist, Inventor, Humanitarian, and Academic

Patricia Bath was born to Rupert and Gladys Bath on November 4, 1942, in New York City.

- Her father was an immigrant from Trinidad, a newspaper columnist.
- Her mother, a descendant of African slaves and Cherokee Native Americans, became a housekeeper.
- She had one brother.

ACCOMPLISHMENTS

- Patricia Bath was the first African American to complete a residency in ophthalmology.
- She was an early pioneer of laser cataract surgery. She invented the Laserphaco Probe for cataract treatment in 1986.
- In 1976, Bath co-founded the American Institute for the Prevention of Blindness.
- She was the first woman elected to the honorary staff of the UCLA Medical Center.
- Patricia Bath was the first African American to serve as a resident in ophthalmology at New York University.
- She was the first African-American woman doctor to receive a patent for a medical purpose. She holds five patents.

EDUCATION

- Hunter College, bachelor of science degree
- Howard University College of Medicine, medical degree

INTERESTING FACTS

The assassination of Martin Luther King Jr. in 1968 caused Bath to dedicate herself to the empowerment of people through the Poor People's Campaign. She organized and led Howard University medical students in providing volunteer health care services. Her primary humanitarian efforts can be seen through her work at The American Institute for the Prevention of Blindness. This organization was founded on the principle that "eyesight is a basic human right." Patricia Bath promoted eye care throughout the globe by providing newborns with free eye drops, vitamins for malnourishment, and vaccinations against diseases that can cause blindness, like measles. Bath spent her time traveling the world performing surgeries, teaching, and lecturing at colleges. Her "personal best moment" happened while in North Africa. There, she restored the sight of a woman who had been blind for over 30 years.

Medicine

DR. JAMES MCCUNE SMITH
1813 - 1865

American Physician, Apothecary, Abolitionist, and Author

James McCune Smith was born to Lavina and Samual Smith on April 18, 1813, in New York City.

- His father was either a freed slave or a white merchant. (Historical facts are unclear)
- James' mother was a former slave.

ACCOMPLISHMENTS

- James McCune Smith became the first African American to receive a medical degree.
- He was a leader, an abolitionist, and a member of the American Anti-Slavery Society, with Frederick Douglass.
- James Smith helped start the National Council of Colored People.
- He practiced as a doctor for nearly 20 years at the Colored Orphan Asylum.
- He wrote the introduction to the Frederick Douglass book, My Bondage and My Freedom.
- Dr. James McCune Smith was one of the most broadly accomplished black intellectuals and activists in antebellum America.
- He was the professor of anthropology at Wilberforce College.

EDUCATION

- New York African Free School, medical degree

- Glasgow University in Scotland, a bachelor's degree, master's degree, and medical degree.

INTERESTING FACTS

James McCune Smith was not able to get a medical degree in the U.S. because of his skin color, so he went to Scotland, where he earned three degrees. While in Scotland, Smith joined the Glasgow Emancipation Society, which helped fund his education. After completing a medical internship in Paris, France, he returned to New York City, where he opened a medical office and a pharmacy that attracted interracial clientele on West Broadway. Smith and his wife were both mixed with African American and European ancestry. Because of racial discrimination, his wife and children passed as white. All of his children married white people, so eventually, they could not tell they had any black ancestors. Smith wrote prolifically about medicine, science, education, racism, and literature.

Medicine

DR. ROBERT BOYD
1855 - 1912

Physician, Apothecary, Abolitionist, and Author

Robert Boyd was born to Maria and Edward Boyd on July 8, 1855, in Giles County, Tennessee.

- He was raised by his mother on a farm.
- His mother brought him to Nashville to live with Paul Eve, a surgeon with an international reputation.

ACCOMPLISHMENTS

- Robert Boyd was the first African-American dentist and doctor to open a practice in Tennessee.
- In 1900, he opened Mercy Hospital, the largest hospital in the South owned and managed by African Americans.
- He became principal of College Grove in Williamson County, Tennessee.
- In 1909, Nashville's second Black-owned bank, People's Savings Bank and Trust Company elected Boyd as its president.
- Dr. Boyd and ten other doctors organized a national fraternity of black doctors called the Society of Colored Physicians and Surgeons.

EDUCATION

- Fisk University, medical degree
- Central
- Tennessee College, medical and dental school degree
- Meharry Medical College, physician, dentist, and professor of clinical medicine
- The University of Chicago, Post-Graduate School of Medicine

INTERESTING FACTS

Robert Boyd was born a slave, eventually living on the plantation of a prominent Tennessee doctor. Boyd dreamed of becoming a physician despite his educational limitations. He discovered that black people in the South had an abnormally high death rate. He then wrote a paper entitled, "What are the Causes of the Great Mortality among Negroes in the Cities of the South, and How is That Mortality to be Lessened?" Around 1893, Boyd ran for mayor and for a seat on the Tennessee General Assembly as a Republican. Dr. Boyd used public forums, including Nashville churches, to help the black public understand the causes, origins, and transmission of tuberculosis, teaching them ways to combat this disease. This organization helped to lower the black mortality rate.

Medicine

LEONIDAS HARRIS BERRY
1902 -1995

Physician, Activist, and Lecturer

Leonidas Harris Berry was born to Beulah Ann and Llewellyn L. Berry on July 20, 1902, in North Carolina.

- His father was a slave who freed himself by fighting in the Civil War. He was the minister of an African Methodist Episcopal Church.
- His mother was a schoolteacher.

ACCOMPLISHMENTS

- Leonidas Berry was an expert in the study of the human stomach and received worldwide acclaim because of his skills and use of the endoscope.
- He was the first medical director of the AME Health Commission.
- Berry was an attending physician at Cook County Hospital.
- He was the first African-American gastroscopist.
- Berry invented the first direct-vision instrument, the gastroscopy scope, to remove diseased tissue in the stomach.
- He lectured worldwide as a representative of several medical associations and societies.
- He authored 15 chapters of Gastrointestinal Panen-doscopy: esophagoscopy, gastroscopy, bulbar and postbulbar duodenoscopy, procto-sigmoidoscopy, colonoscopy, and peritoneoscopy, a technical, instructional work.

EDUCATION

- Wilberforce University, bachelor of science
- University of Chicago bachelor of science
- Rush Medical College of the University of Chicago, medical degree
- Graduate School of Medicine at the University of Illinois, M.S. degree in pathology

INTERESTING FACTS

Berry worked to help combat drug use. He became a world-renowned physician who dedicated his life to the pursuit of racial, physical, and economic parity for African Americans in Chicago through medicine, teaching, writing, lecturing, and community service. When evaluating illnesses, Berry examined the physical and economic causes rather than the color of his patient's skin. Berry produced several books, video recordings, and films to illustrate the study of the stomach and other organs affected by digestive disorders.

Medicine

JOCELYN ELDERS
1933 - ____

Physician, Activist, and Lecturer

Joceyln Elders was born to Haller and Curtis Jones on August 13, 1933, in Arkansas.

- She had seven siblings.
- The family lived in a poor, segregated area of Schaal, Arkansas.

ACCOMPLISHMENTS

- Jocelyn Elders was the first African American to serve as the U.S. Surgeon General.
- Elders joined the Army and trained in physical therapy at the Brooke Army Medical Center.
- Elders spoke of the dangers of pregnancy with her patients and distributed contraceptives to limit those dangers.
- Elders campaigned for expanded sex education throughout Arkansas and was the first African American and the second woman to head the U.S. Public Health Service.
- Elders combined her clinical practice with research in pediatric endocrinology, publishing over 100 papers.
- She received both The Woman of Distinction and Arkansas Democrat Woman of the Year awards.

EDUCATION

- Philander Smith College, bachelor of arts degree
- The University of Arkansas, medical degree

INTERESTING FACTS

Jocelyn Elders' birth name was Minnie Jones. She took the name Jocelyn in college. She grew up in a segregated town with her seven siblings, working the cotton fields. They lived in a three-room cabin with no indoor toilet and no electricity. Jocelyn's grandmother encouraged her to read books. Her family picked extra cotton to earn the $3.43 for her bus fare to college. She was the first to attend. Elders, who had never met a doctor until she was sixteen, realized that she wanted to be one. After graduating from college, she joined the U.S. Army's Women's Medical Specialist Corps. As U.S. Surgeon General, Elders worked to reduce teen pregnancy. She was also focused on tobacco use, national health care, Acquired Immune Deficiency Syndrome (AIDS), gun control, and drug and alcohol abuse. Elders dealt with several scandals because of her views on sex education. The Clinton administration later asked her to step down as Surgeon General. She is a public speaker who continues to champion better national health care.

Medicine

MARY ELIZA MAHONEY
1845 - 1926

Nurse

Mary Eliza Mahoney's exact day of birth is unknown, but she was born in 1845 in Boston, Massachusetts.

- Her parents were free blacks from the south who moved north before the Civil War.
- She had two siblings.

ACCOMPLISHMENTS

- She was a member of the National Association of Colored Graduate Nurses (NACGN),
- NACGN established the Mary Mahoney Award in 1936.
- Mahoney delivered a powerful speech at the first NACGN Convention at Boston in 1909 and was made a lifetime member
- Mahoney was inducted into the Nursing Hall of Fame in 1976 and received induction into the National Women's Hall of Fame in 1993.
- She became the director of a black orphanage in New York.

EDUCATION

- New England Hospital for Women and Children, nursing degree

INTERESTING FACTS

Supplementing her low income, Mary Eliza Mahoney worked as a janitor at the New England Hospital for Women and Children. Mary Mahoney was widely recognized within her field as a pioneer who opened the door of opportunity for many black women interested in the nursing profession. Mahoney was a part of the Women's Suffrage Movement. She has been credited as one of the first women to register to vote in Boston following the ratification of the 19th Amendment. She never married and instead dedicated herself to her work.

Finance

Finance

NORMAN L. MCGHEE SR.
1897 - 1979

Licensed Stock Dealer and Brokerage Firm Founder

Norman L. McGhee Sr. was born to Maidee and Daniel McGhee on November 20, 1897, in Austell, Georgia.

- His father was an AME minister.
- He was married and had four children.

ACCOMPLISHMENTS

- In 1952, Normal L. McGhee Sr. founded McGhee & Company, the first black-owned firm to be licensed by the National Association of Securities Dealers.
- He was the editor for The Cleveland Post, a weekly newspaper in Ohio.
- McGhee founded his own real estate company, Citizen's Realty Management. The majority of his clients were black.
- He encouraged black people to engage in the "American industrial system" by investing in stocks.
- He established a mutual investment fund, Everyman's Fund, primarily for the black community.

EDUCATION

- Howard University, bachelor of arts degree, law degree

INTERESTING FACTS

Norman McGhee lived in the Atlanta suburbs in a majority white middle-class neighborhood. After graduating from college, he moved to Ohio to escape discrimination in the south. The Great Depression devastated many American lives and businesses, but Norman McGhee saw this as an opportunity. He founded Citizen's Realty Management Company and began investing in real estate. At one point, his company owned more than 1000 properties. He often traveled to the YWCA to offer investment courses and became known as the "Wizard of Wall Street." Norman McGhee remained active in civic organizations, including being a trustee of Wilberforce University, the oldest private historically black university in the U.S., owned and operated by African Americans.

Finance

MAGGIE LENA WALKER
1864 - 1934

Entrepreneur, Bank Owner, Teacher

Maggie Lena Draper was born to Elizabeth Draper and Eccles Cuthbert on July 15, 1864

- Her mother was formerly enslaved and a cook for Elizabeth Van Lew, an abolitionist on whose estate Maggie was born.
- Her father was an Irish-born Confederate soldier who met her mother on the Van Lew estate. They were never married.
- Shortly after Maggie's birth, her mother married William Mitchell, the butler of the estate.

ACCOMPLISHMENTS

- Maggie Lena Walker was the first woman (of any race) to own a bank in the United States.
- She served as president of St. Luke Penny Savings Bank, the first African-American woman in the United States to do so.
- Maggie Lena Walker was grand secretary of the Independent Order of St. Luke, one of the largest African-American fraternal benefit societies dedicated to the social and financial advancement of African Americans.
- She held leadership positions with the National Association of Colored Women (NACW) and the Richmond chapter of the National Association for the Advancement of Colored People (NAACP).

EDUCATION

- Richmond Colored Normal School, education degree

INTERESTING FACTS

After graduating, Maggie Lena Walker taught at Lancaster School and remained there until 1886, when she married Armstead Walker Jr., a brick contractor. She was forced to leave her job due to the school's policy against married teachers. When few African Americans could deposit their money in a financial institution, Maggie Lena Walker established a bank that allowed the black community to save and receive credit. St. Luke Penny Savings Bank was widely successful and survived the Great Depression, later merging with other banks. As the bank president, she was known for giving loans to black business owners and residents at fair rates. She was quoted as saying, "Let us have a bank that will take the nickels and turn them into dollars." Maggie Lena Walker's house in Richmond, Virginia, has since been designated a National Historic Site by the National Park Service.

Finance

PHYLLIS ANN WALLACE
1921 - 1993

Economist and Activist

Phyllis Ann Wallace was born Annie Rebecca Wallace to Stevella and Johan Wallace in Baltimore, Maryland, on June 9, 1921.

- Her father was a craftsman.
- She had seven siblings.

ACCOMPLISHMENTS

- Phyllis Ann Wallace was the first woman to receive a doctorate of economics at Yale University.
- She became a voice for anti-discrimination in the workplace and was an important part of the anti-workplace-discrimination contingencies of the Civil Rights Act of 1964.
- With her expertise in economics, she conducted studies on underemployment in the African-American community and how it affected the labor market.
- She worked to resolve economic issues with urban minority youth.
- Phyllis Ann Wallace received several awards for her accomplishments, including the National Economic Association's Westerfield Award.

EDUCATION

- New York University, bachelor's degree in economics (graduating magna cum laude)
- Yale University, master's degree and PhD

INTERESTING FACTS

Phyllis Ann Wallace joined the Equal Employment Opportunity Commission, which investigates employee allegations of workplace discrimination, and spearheaded the research for the commission's gender and race discrimination petition against AT&T. As a result, AT&T came to an agreement and paid millions in back pay, wage adjustments, and other benefits related to past discriminatory practices. The EEOC called the agreement "the largest and most comprehensive civil-rights settlement ever reached in the United States."

Finance

ABRAM LINCOLN HARRIS
1899 - 1963

Economist, Academic, Anthropologist, and Writer

Abram Lincoln Harris was born to Mary and Abram Lincoln Harris Sr. in Richmond, Virginia on January 17, 1899.

- His father was a butcher.
- His mother was a teacher.

ACCOMPLISHMENTS

- Abram Lincoln Harris, Jr., the grandson of slaves, was the first nationally recognized black economist.
- He wrote a dissertation on African-American labor, telling the complete story of Black Americans' participation in the "American labor market."
- Abram Lincoln Harris also wrote and published The Negro as Capitalist, which traced the role of black people in the development of capitalism from slavery to independent business and bank ownership.

EDUCATION

- Virginia Union University, bachelor of science degree
- University of Pittsburgh, master of arts degree
- Columbia University, doctorate in economics

INTERESTING FACTS

Abram Lincoln Harris held many service jobs, including Pullman porter and shipyard worker. He attended college when only a small share of African Americans had access to higher education. He produced groundbreaking work revealing the important role African Americans played in the history of the U.S. economy. Abram Lincoln Harris became a professor and educated the next generation of students interested in economics as a professor at Howard University, a historically black college in Washington, D.C., and then at the University of Chicago.

Finance

JOSEPH L. SEARLES III
1942 - 2021

Lawyer, Businessman, Football Player, and Community Administrator

Joseph L. Searles III was born on January 2, 1942, in Fort Hood, Texas.

ACCOMPLISHMENTS

- Joseph L. Searles III became the first black floor member and floor broker in the New York Stock Exchange.
- He worked as a floor partner in the firm of Neuberger, Loeb and Company.
- Joseph L. Searles III is one of the early urban development specialists credited with using mainstream strategies to transform the size and quality of minority business ventures.
- He was a member of the exclusive Stock Exchange Luncheon Club.

EDUCATION

- Kansas State University, bachelor's degree in political science
- George Washington University Law School, law degree

INTERESTING FACTS

Joseph L. Searles III grew up in a military family. He played football at Kansas State University and later professionally with the New York Giants. He was among the few blacks in the National Football League (NFL) during the Civil Rights Era and was paid a salary of $14,000. He was asked to cut his hair and hide his Jaguar when arriving to practice, fearing some would retaliate because of his success. Considered a leading expert on urban retailing, he was a member of the development team for "Harlem USA" and was a partner in the $141,000,000.00 retail/entertainment project in Washington, D.C. called "D.C. USA."

Finance

VALERIE MOSLEY
1960 - ___

Financial Executive and Investment Firm Founder

Valerie Mosley was born to Clara and Clarence Mosley on February 5, 1960, in Tuskegee, Alabama.

- She has three children.

✷ ACCOMPLISHMENTS

- Valerie Mosley is the founder of Valmo Ventures, Inc., which specializes in trend identification, global wealth management, and corporate advisory.
- She held positions at multiple Wall Street firms, including senior vice president, partner, and portfolio manager for Wellington Management Company, a global investment firm.
- During her twenty-year career, she handled over $20 billion in fixed income portfolios for corporate and public pension funds, endowments, and mutual funds.

✷ EDUCATION

- Duke University bachelor of arts degree
- University of Pennsylvania's Wharton School of Finance M.B.A. degree

✷ INTERESTING FACTS

Valerie Mosley served on President Barack Obama's Board of Advisors on Historically Black Colleges and Universities. She also served on the Federal Reserve Bank of Boston's Advisory Board for Diversity. Valerie Mosley was named one of the "50 Most Powerful Women in Business" in 2006, as one of the "Top 75 Blacks on Wall Street" by Black Enterprise magazine in 2011, and one of the "Top 50 African Americans on Wall Street" by Black Enterprise. With the goal of impacting future generations, she developed a financial literacy program for high school students.

Finance

MADAM C. J. WALKER
1867 - 1919

Entrepreneur, Philanthropist, and Activist

CJ Walker was born Sarah Breedlove to Minerva and Owen, on December 23, 1867, close to Delta, Louisiana.

- She was one of six children.
- She was the first of her siblings born into freedom.

✸ ACCOMPLISHMENTS

- Madam CJ Walker was the first female self-made millionaire, selling haircare and beauty products.
- Between 1911 and 1919, CJ Walker and her company employed several thousand women as sales agents for its products and trained nearly 20,000 women.
- She delivered lectures on political, economic, and social issues at conventions sponsored by powerful black institutions.
- She made financial donations to numerous organizations.
- Madame Walker's lavish estate served as a social gathering place for African Americans.

✸ EDUCATION

- CJ Walker did not receive a formal education. She was trained and worked for Annie Malone, a successful haircare entrepreneur.

✸ INTERESTING FACTS

Orphaned at the age of seven, Sarah moved to Vicksburg, Mississippi, at the age of ten. As was common among black women of her time, Sarah suffered severe dandruff and other scalp ailments, including baldness. She first learned about haircare from her brothers, who were barbers. After she became famous, her husband encouraged her to use the more recognizable name "Madam C.J. Walker," by which she was thereafter known. She showed other black women how to budget and build their own businesses. She also encouraged them to become financially independent. After her death, her daughter took over the company, and their products are still sold today.

Finance

ANTHONY OVERTON
1865 - 1946

Banker and Manufacturer

- Anthony Overton was born to Martha and Anthony Overton Sr. on March 21, 1865, in Monroe, Louisiana

- His father was born into slavery and later emancipated by Abraham Lincoln.

ACCOMPLISHMENTS

- Anthony Overton was the first African American to become a major business mogul.

- He opened the Chicago Bee Newspaper and was the first to hire a woman editor. He also founded Victory Life Insurance Company and Douglass National Bank, the second nationally chartered black-owned bank in the United States.

- Anthony Overton opened a grocery store that sold the nationally known High Brown Face Powder, which was "the first market success in the sale of cosmetics for black women."

EDUCATION

- Washburn College, bachelor's degree in chemistry

- University of Kansas, legal degree

INTERESTING FACTS

Anthony Overton practiced law for a time and even served as a judge before developing his business operations. His building, The Overton Hygienic Building, was later known in history as the Palace Hotel. The building is now owned by another company, which announced plans to use it as an incubator for small businesses. The National Association for the Advancement of Colored People (NAACP) awarded Anthony Overton the Spingarn Medal for outstanding achievement by an African American.

Finance

LAUREN SIMMONS
1994 - ____

Businesswoman, Motivational Speaker, and Film Producer

- Lauren Simmons was born on August 11, 1994, in Georgia.

ACCOMPLISHMENTS

- At 22 years old, Lauren Simmons shattered the glass ceiling by being the youngest and only full-time female equity trader on Wall Street for Rosenblatt Securities. Affectionately dubbed as the "Lone Woman On Wall Street," Simmons was also the second African-American woman in history to sport the prestigious badge.
- With a pass rate of only 20%, Lauren Simmons passed the Series 19 exam after studying for just one month.
- She was hired as an equity trader by Rosenblatt Securities.

EDUCATION

- Kennesaw State University, bachelor's degree in genetics and statistics

INTERESTING FACTS

Lauren Simmons originally aspired to become a genetic counselor. She decided against this and instead became interested in becoming an equity trader on Wall Street. To do her part to ensure that more young people who look like her feel seen in the financial services field, she is producing a film about her journey at the New York Stock Exchange. Lauren received endorsements from Invisalign, Ford Motor Company, Club Pilates, and LinkedIn. She is actively working on her first publication focused on women and millennials in finance.

Finance

JAMILA SOUFFRANT
1984 - ____

Financial Podcast Host and Blogger

Jamila Souffrant was born in Jamaica

- She is married.
- She and her husband have three children.

ACCOMPLISHMENTS

- Jamila Souffrant is the host of the Journey to Launch podcast and blog.
- She is a Certified Financial Education Instructor (CFEI)
- With a background in personal finance, she decided to share her own journey by blogging. Two years later, she created the podcast.
- She has been featured in Essence, Refinery 29, Money Magazine, CNBC, CBS, and Business Insider.

EDUCATION

- Certified Financial Education Instructor

INTERESTING FACTS

Jamila Souffrant purchased her first real estate property right out of college, at the age of 22. She and her husband saved an astonishing $169,000 in two years. She is considered a go-to financial thought leader in the personal finance field and is the resident financial expert on a weekly segment on News 12. Jamila works with clients to teach them how to save, invest, and retire.

50

CPSIA information can be obtained
at www.ICGtesting.com
Printed in the USA
BVHW012017191222
654360BV00018B/67